A Thing of Beauty Is a Joy Forever

Volume II

A Beginner's Guide to Becoming an Antiques Dealer

Christine Pym

Strategic Book Publishing and Rights Co.

All background information and photographic imagery supplied courtesy of David J Pym Antiques, Newbury, Berkshire, United Kingdom (davidjpym.com)

Strategic Book Publishing and Rights Co., LLC
USA | Singapore
www.sbpra.net

For information about special discounts for bulk purchases, please contact Strategic Book Publishing and Rights Co. Special Sales, at bookorder@sbpra.net.

ISBN: 978-1-68235-670-8

Book Design: Suzanne Kelly

A thing of beauty is a joy for ever:
Its loveliness increases; it will never
Pass into nothingness

John Keats
1795–1821

Dedication

I wish to dedicate this book to the memory of my late dear mother, Margaret Jean Cowley, neé Taylor (1929 - 2015) proud resident and upstanding citizen of Royal Wootton Bassett in Wiltshire, UK.

Preface

THERE IS STILL A HUGE aura of mystery and intrigue surrounding the subject of antiques, so much so that it continues to command prime viewing spots on daytime television and seems to harness and appeal to the very heart of our innate nature to want to return to basic bargaining, the primeval and tribal trading tradition of ancient civilisations. This is especially the case at the basic ground-roots level. Perhaps that is due to the fact that it is still specifically an uncategorised and unregulated industry. It appears, despite some dedicated university projects and studies, that not one body or organisation has been able to 'get to the bottom of it.' How long is a piece of string? The subject has no beginning and no end and is constantly changing. Although, having said that, the antiques dealer profession is now specifically listed by the Careers Advisory Service and UCAS as a career option and not just hidden behind closed doors, as it once seemed, for only a select few. Also, there appear to be many different subsidiary services/trades such as up-working or redesigning redundant furniture and household effects destined for the skip-and-restoration services. There is no doubt that a revamped retro or antique item mixed into a modern or period interior will provide a totally authentic and eclectic mood.

For myself, having worked directly within the industry for the past 30 years, I can definitely disagree with one generalised view, however, which is that it does not require any qualifications. That may be the case at general entry, but forging a long-term career path, it's quite to the contrary. Basic instincts are one thing, but actually maintaining a viable business, entirely something else.

Table of Contents

Introduction

IN THE FIRST VOLUME, *A Beginner's Guide to Becoming an Antiques Dealer*, there were general suggestions of how and where to start an antiques business as a hobby or a part-time or full-time business, together with specific rules and regulations of the industry. The aim of this book is to extend and elaborate with insider tips and pointers regarding operation and set-up. However, it would seem expedient in the first instance to explore some of the artefacts currently available in the marketplace. These are items which mainly come from house clearances and probate, quite often Victoriana, ephemera and artefacts which were mass produced to satisfy the new working man's desire to decorate new homes with curios, collections and automatons before the advent of radio and television.

With efforts to try to simplify the situation somewhat, these artefacts can be divided into some broader, generalised groups as described in Section I.

Historically, many dedicated antique dealers have learnt their trade over a number of years, possibly working as a porter in an auction house or an assistant in an antiques shop or establishment, the idea being that they will learn and build a wide general knowledge of variety of their antiques and pricing by handling and viewing objects as they come through the door and are sold, presumably, at market price. Some people may also have taken a degree course in art appreciation, art history or fine arts history, especially if they wish to work at the higher, more specialised level where seasoned antiques from important country estates may still be traded together with serious art. The values of such items can be speculative but require intense research, authentication and verification.

However, in essence, an antiques business is a form of retail with a twist, the twist being that instead of establishing business liaisons with wholesale goods companies of a preferred nature and ordering specific products directly from them, the potential

G. Duvernet 'Oblivion' Rare Bronze c1925

Goldscheider 'Butterfly Girl' c1930

'Lions' Japanese Meiji period Bronze c1895

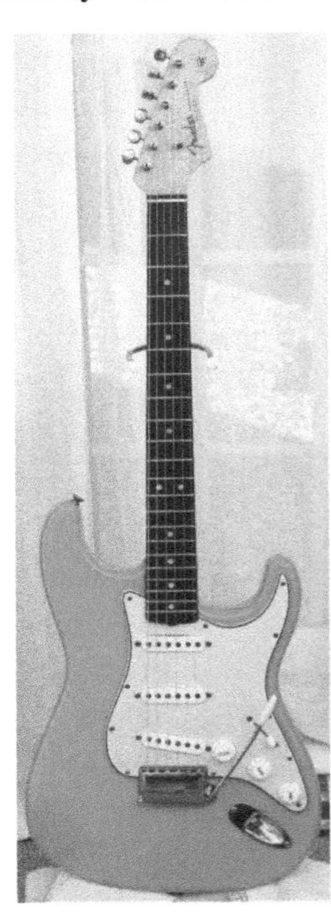

Fender Stratocaster Custom Colour Fiesta Red 1964

buying ground is vast, unspecified and unquantifiable in terms of value and available artefacts which need to be individually sourced, researched and purchased.

An individual person's previous work experience, skills and expertise all come into play together with financial standing in terms of investment and self-sufficiency. Indeed, it is often the case that a retired person might enter the industry to begin with, possibly on a part-time basis. On the other hand, it is perfectly feasible that a successful business can be built at an earlier age as a professional career. It should not be thought, however, that this is in any way an easy career path. Rewarding? Yes, by virtue of being able to work in one's own business with beautiful, intriguing and heritage items and having the chance to own them, if often only fleetingly, as tools of the trade.

There is also, potentially, the lure of gold and riches, but with a prerequisite for flair, self-sufficiency and quite often living on one's own wits. A certain *je ne sais quoi* air, at all times challenging, the industry will stretch and engage all aspects of one's persona and sense of survival. And for that very reason, personal circumstances will quite often dictate an individual's level of involvement and risk. With the latter in mind, what better route than a step-by-step, direct hands-on approach?

Hence, there will be some business tips and pointers in Section II.

SECTION I

Product Information

LIST OF ANTIQUE STYLES AND PERIODS

1. Medieval
2. Renaissance
3. Tudor
4. Elizabethan
5. Rococo
6. Baroque
7. Queen Anne
8. Georgian
9. Regency
10. William IV
11 Victorian
12. Arts and Crafts
13. Art Nouveau
14. Edwardian
15. Art Deco
16. Retro
17. Swinging '60s
18. Modernist
19. Contemporary

Fine gilded metal and marble 8-day mantel timepiece with 'swinging cherub' pendulum and spring-driven movement

8 day drop-pendulum wall clock

8 day fusee dial clock

1.1 ANTIQUE CLOCKS

An antique or vintage timepiece can invariably set the mood and style of a house. It is often considered the 'heartbeat,' providing a relaxing, gentle and melodious tick or chime as well as a unique character and presence, usually positioned at the hearth or mantel. There are various styles following similar authentic lines, but the important feature is that it will have stood the test of time and be a reliable worker, hopefully. However, that is invariably the problem, because although many people will have inherited an antique timepiece, a large number are no longer working. There are several reasons for this: either it did not have a quality movement designed for longevity, it has developed a mechanical problem, or it simply needs a thorough overhaul, clean and reset.

Since time is of the essence more than ever today, there seem to be less horological specialists to hand in high streets and towns, generally. In fact, it has been estimated that only two hundred and fifty dedicated professionals currently exist in the UK, which is in complete contrast to earlier centuries when most towns and villages would have had one or several clockmakers, and they were considered to be master craftsmen. Most modern clockmakers only repair modern clocks, which is because the majority of timepieces are now factory-made. Therefore, the skilled artisan antique clock specialists who repair individually engineered older timepieces are generally employed by jewellers or antique shops.

It is a complex trade requiring fine motor coordination, precision, knowledge of small gears and fine machinery, and the ability to read and decipher blueprints and instructions for a vast range of antique to modern styles. The skills and tools required to repair watches are completely different. Therefore, it is a separate field requiring another specialist.

The original term *clockmaker* is said to date from around 1390, about a century after the first mechanical timepieces appeared, which were thought to have been devised by monks to relay prayer times. Then, from the 15th to 17th centuries, the skill was considered leading edge and the most technically

THOMAS TOMPION

'The famous Tompion 'Q' Clock was commissioned for Queen Mary in 1693 by her husband King William III. It is a 7.5 inch miniature quarter-repeating miniature table clock with silver heraldry mounts and one of a pair, the other identical owned by King William III. This particular clock was thought to have passed out of royal hands possibly on the Queen's death in 1694 or later the King's in 1706.

It was recently sold at Auction on 24th June 2019, achieving 1.93 million pounds total with premium and thought to be the World's most expensive clock ever sold.'

advanced trade in existence. Clockmakers also developed scientific equipment, and even the first harmonica was said to have been introduced by a German artisan and later mass-produced by Matthias Hohner.

Early clockmakers then were considered to be important master craftsmen, and one such leading name, if not the (English) leading name and most revered is Thomas Tompion.

Thomas Tompion (1639–1713) was born in Northill, Bedfordshire, England, and is still regarded by many, to this day, as the father of English clockmaking. He was a clockmaker, watchmaker and mechanic whose work includes some of the most historic and important clocks and watches in the world and, not surprisingly, his timepieces can command very high prices, if and when any outstanding examples appear at auction.

His esteemed excellence and unrivalled reputation throughout the world is based on sound design as well as the use of high-quality materials. He also employed workmen and apprentices with outstanding skills. Many such employees had French and Dutch Huguenot origins—for example, Daniel and Nicholas Delander, Henri Callot, and Charles Molyns.

In 1676, King Charles II established the new Royal Observatory and appointed Tompion to create two identical clocks for the wall of the Octagon Room, based on an idea from the scientist Robert Hooke, with whom Tompion had become associated. The clocks had a very long pendulum swinging in a very small arc and were driven by a dead-beat escapement. They only needed to be wound once a year and proved so very accurate that they were instrumental in achieving the correct calculations needed for astronomical observations.

Many of his clocks are still operational today, and there are two further examples of his one-year timepieces at Buckingham Palace. Some of his most prominent and pioneering examples of English horology are in situ in prime museums all over the country.

It is estimated that during his illustrious career he built about 5,500 watches and 650 clocks, the latter particularly known for their robust construction and ingenuity of design. We are only touching briefly here upon such an important name in master craftsmanship history, Thomas Tompion, a name so important, in fact, that upon his death in 1713, he was buried in Westminster Abbey, later followed by his partner and former apprentice George Graham in 1751. A plaque also commemorates both of their clock-making achievements by being permanently situated at their original workshop site in Fleet Street, London.

Many, if not all, of Tompion's' partners, such as Edward Banger, partner in 1701, as well as apprentices George Allett, Henry Callowe (Callot), Daniel Delander, Richard Emes, Ambrose Garner, Obadiah Gardner, William Graham (nephew of George Graham), George Harrison, Whitestone Littlemore, Jeremiah Martin, Charles Molin (Molyns), William Mourlay, Charles Murray, Robert Pattison, William Sherwood, Richard Street, Charles Symson, William Thompson, James Tunn, and Thomas White all became important makers and workmen in their own right and are names to note and look out for.

If ever we are lucky enough to encounter such wonderful masterpieces, or indeed any existing timepieces from the 16th, 17th or even 18th centuries, even from the early 19th century and early Georgian Regency periods, such timepieces with such names are somewhat rarities to be found, especially in good working order and condition.

English longcase clocks dating from the early 1600s are the most readily available, or should one say the longest and oldest reliable historic survivors. The long pendulum and movements have proved to be responsible for their longevity and reliability.

Antique clockmaker's names can be researched on the internet, giving details such as their trading addresses and work span, and there are various publications available recording both clock and watchmakers. The Horological Foundation, in particular, provides some extensive information in this regard.

From the early 1820s, factory-produced mechanisms and escapements were becoming more readily available, and names inscribed on the clock face were not necessarily those of makers but more often that of the retailer or primary owning organisation. For example, those from British Rail, the Royal Air Force, the Royal Navy, and the General Post Office are all collected in their own right. There were also prominent timepieces in schools and other public places such as town halls.

Following on from this, standards of factory-produced mechanisms up to about the 1930s were high and timepieces still complex, requiring precision and engineering. Therefore, out of these 19th-century and early-20th-century models, the quality and degree of manufacture will determine the overall continued working condition and reliability.

Sadly, as already mentioned, some clocks may be deemed unfit or too expensive, in terms of the clock's overall intrinsic value, for repair or restoration. Alternatively, a special family heirloom may be restored but at a price far exceeding the clock's value and worth, which can only be ascertained by obtaining valuations. In cases where an antique clock is one of a kind or requires a special piece, a skilled, modern-day antique clock repairer would either be able to construct a suitable replacement part himself, or there may be a specialist trade supplier available for him to contact.

1.2 MIRRORS AND LOOKING GLASSES

A mirror is an object that reflects light in such a way that, for incident light in some range of wavelengths, the reflected light preserves many or most of the detailed characteristics of the original light. This is different from other light-reflecting objects that do not preserve much of the original wave signal other than colour and diffuse reflected light.

Mirrors are commonly used for personal grooming or admiring oneself, in which case the archaic term 'looking-glass' is sometimes still used. They are also used as decorative items and in architecture and interior design. This is where one's imagination and style can fully take charge, as they come in all shapes, forms and styles and can be used to effectively 'enlarge'

Maria Gunning

'18th Century 7ft vanity mirror owned by Maria Gunning, former Countess of Coventry, who was a renowned society beauty who reportedly made men faint in awe of her beauty. This peer/vanity mirror was given to her by her husband, the 6th Earl of Coventry. Unfortunately, Maria died at age 27 in 1760, due to lead and mercury poisoning caused by the makeup she loved and wore at the time to make her appearance white-skinned which was considered fashionable and which had also been suspected responsible at the time of death of Elizabeth I in 1603. The mirror was housed at the family seat at Croome Park in Worcestershire for nearly 200 years until 1948 when it was first sold and then at a later auction it is reported to have made in excess of £300,000.'

a room or provide a focal adornment—for example, above a mantelpiece (an over mantle).

Although there are some ancient images recording ladies admiring themselves in looking glasses as early as 6000 BC, and various recordings of some crude versions in Roman times and later in the Renaissance, it was not until the 16th century that Venetian glassmakers on the island of Murano invented the plate-glass method, using a backing of mercury, that a near-perfect, undistorted reflection was achieved. For over one hundred years, the Murano factory supplied and installed mirrors in richly decorated frames as lavish luxury decorative items to palaces all over Europe.

Eventually, the formula of the mercury process was leaked and stolen due to industrial espionage, and the 'secret' arrived in London and Paris during the 17th century. This then resulted in large-scale industrialisation and production in French workshops and eventually widespread manufacture of affordable mirrors for the masses. However, the toxicity of mercury remained a problem. The invention of the silvered-glass mirror is accredited to German chemist Justus von Liebig, in 1835. His process involved the deposition of a thin layer of metallic silver onto glass through the chemical reduction of silver nitrate. This paved the way for cheaper mass productions up to modern times when glass mirrors are most often coated with silver or aluminium, implemented by a series of coatings.

Generally speaking, then, the older the mirror, the most lavishly decorative and evocative the frame but the worse the condition or reflective quality of the glass is likely to be. Some wonderful examples of baroque, rococo or gilt gesso mirrors can still be found, but quite often the glass (mirror) is very dark, non-reflective, pitted or worn, so they are more evocative of a style and period for decorative purposes rather than for use as a looking glass. The glass may then, and will in some cases, be changed for a modern version, but inevitably its overall appearance will be too bland, lack character, and not be in keeping with the original. The price too will usually reflect such a modernisation. The optimum find in that case will be a period frame, as small or large as one likes, with the original quality glass still intact.

Of course, the prices of these stunning masterpieces, which usually have exotically carved and gilded frames, can easily reach four- or five-figure sums, dependent on their overall condition and appearance. There are some magnificent, virtually full-scale, wall-size, 19th-century versions periodically appearing for sale at auction.

1.3 CHERUBS, PUTTI AND ANGELS

Putti, cherubs and angels are popular mystical and romantic iconology associated with antiques. Their appearance seems to immediately denote romanticism and mystique from the past, probably because they can be found in both religious and secular art from the 1420s in Italy to the turn of the 16th century in the Netherlands and Germany, the Mannerist period and the late Renaissance in France, and throughout baroque ceiling frescoes.

They also experienced a major revival in the 19th century in French paintings, in particular. So many artists have depicted them that a list would be pointless, but among the best known are the sculptor Donatello and the painter Raphael. The two relaxed and curious putti who appear at the foot of Raphael's Sistine Madonna are often reproduced, and they can sometimes be seen to adorn tombs and sarcophagi throughout history.

A putto (plural, putti) is a figure in a work of art depicted as a chubby male child, usually nude and sometimes winged. They are commonly confused with, and yet completely unrelated to, cherubim which traditionally have four faces of different species and several pairs of wings and were biblical angels. However, in the baroque period of art, the putto came to represent the omnipresence of God.

A putto representing a cupid is also called an 'amorino.' This form of putto was derived in various ways through Greek and Roman mythology, Amor/Cupid being the god of love and companion of Aphrodite or Venus. When depicted in this case, in the ancient classical world of art, they appeared as winged infants and were believed to influence human lives.

One more poignant and emotive symbolism of a cupid is as a commemorative keepsake of an individual, in particular reflecting the high infant mortality in the 17th and 18th centuries.

Putto and cupid adorn-ments on wood carvings and appliqués on silver have appeared and resurfaced throughout the different time periods, particularly in the late 19th and early 20th centuries. Their beauty, as in art, is marvelled and reflected, as too are the different religious interpretations. It is this intrinsic unique artistry and skill of the craftsman which encapsulates and personifies such fascinating symbols of bygone eras. They are definitely romantic embellishments and symbolisms to look out for.

1.4 CHANDELIERS AND LIGHTING

Another symbol of romanticism and bygone days is probably the chandelier, especially as the earliest types designed specifically for candles were used by the wealthy in medieval times and could be moved from one room to another within a house.

From the 15th century, more complex forms based on ring or crown designs became popular decorative features in palaces and homes of nobility, clergy and merchants. High costs made them a symbol of luxury and status. By the early 18th century, ornate cast ormolu forms with long, curved arms and many candles appeared in the homes of large numbers of the growing merchant class.

Various Antique bespoke chandeliers

Neoclassical motifs became an increasingly common element, mostly in cast metals but also in carved and gilded wood. Then, later, developments in glassmaking allowed cheaper production of lead crystal, where the light-scattering and reflective properties of the glass made it a popular form and led eventually to the crystal chandelier.

More complex and elaborate chandeliers continued to be developed throughout the 18th and 19th centuries, particularly by Bohemians and Venetian glassmakers, who were both masters in the art. Bohemian styles were largely successful across Europe, and their biggest draw was the spectacular light refraction that could be obtained due to facets and bevels of crystal prisms. As a reaction to this new taste, Italian glass factories in Murano also created new kinds of artistic light sources. Typical features of a Murano chandelier are the intricate arabesques of leaves, flowers and fruits that would be enriched by coloured glass. An incredible amount of skill and time was required to precisely twist and shape a chandelier of this type, and so it was most commonly used in huge forms to light theatres and rooms in important palaces.

In the mid-19th century, as gas lighting appeared, some candle chandeliers were converted, and by the 1890s, following the invention of electricity, some chandeliers used a combination of both gas and electricity. Others were fitted with bulbs shaped to imitate candle flames; some had bulbs containing a shimmering gas discharge. Then, towards the end of the 19th century, chandeliers were often used purely as decorative focal points for rooms and often did not illuminate. Their appeal had been devalued generally as a status symbol. However, smaller and less elaborate crystal styles were popular in the early 1900s until the 1940s and 1950s for more general household adornment. Predominantly, it is these forms which have survived today, albeit missing perhaps one or two faceted drops and with some modification.

In modern households of the 21st century, these amazing antique creations, especially when restored, have been revived once again to evoke a sense of glamour, opulence and style.

1.5 ART DECO LADY-STYLE LAMPS

Stylised, sometimes athletic, poses and partially or scantily clad forms are particularly desirable today, finished in cold-painted silver or gold over spelter and each lady figure holding a hand-made marbled or crackled globe. A large number were designed by or attributed to Josef Lorenzl, who was a very well-known sculptor and designer from the 1920s to 1940s art deco period and also made bronze 'lady-

Art Deco 'Lady Style' Lamps

'Lorenzl' Cold-Painted Bronze C1929

figure,' cold-painted statues. Both art forms were particularly risqué at the time but managed to escape censorship due to their beautiful artistic poses, stylisation and quality of manufacture.

Unfortunately, only a limited number have survived in good condition, and hence the price for such an original item with hand-formed and blown shade quite often commands a four-figure price tag! Here at davidjpym.com, we still endeavour to keep a good stock, as much as availability dictates, of these iconic emblems, as too, original Rene Lalique art glass, which then becomes our next section.

1.6 ART NOUVEAU AND ART DECO ART GLASS

René Jules Lalique was featured in Volume I of A Beginner's Guide and has remained popular for the last nine years since and will most likely remain forever, as his name is etched in history as a master art nouveau and art deco jeweller and forerunner and purveyor of exquisite artistry, design and technique in stylised early-20th-century art glass. Many important rare, original pieces have been sold by us, and we still hold a substantial stock of fine-quality, investment-grade car mascots, perfume bottles and bespoke vases.

Most people will be aware of the unique opalescence which is his particular trademark and exists in many of his creations until his death in 1945, when the 'secret' of its creation was not passed onto his son, Marc, as he was, of course, totally unaware of how popular and famous his specialist wares would become. It was the most he could do, during the Second World War, to maintain and protect the business. The moulds are still used today by the Lalique Factory, courtesy of having been successfully preserved and spirited away by the fantastic efforts of the grand master. Post-1945 Lalique glass is still produced using some of the moulds but with different types of glass and techniques.

Daum, Gallé, Moser and Tiffany are also important and popular names from this period.

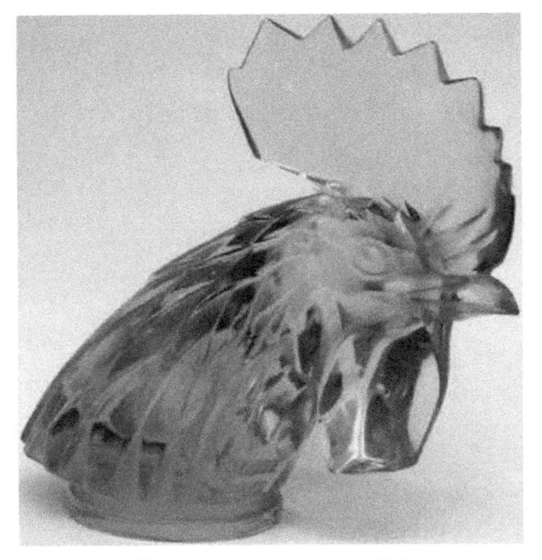

'Tete de Coq' car mascot c1928

'R Lalique 'Sauterelles', rare vase c1912'

'R Lalique 'Petit Moineau' 'Head Up' and 'Tail Down' Frosted Grey c1928

'R Lalique 'Cameret' vase c1928'

'WMF Bespoke Claret Jug and six glasses decorated with green shamrock motif, c1900

1.7 WMF

You know it—we all know it now—the famous Wurttembergische Metallwarenfabrik, or the Wurttemberg Metalware Company, famous for their fabulous quality late-Victorian, and specifically the 1905 catalogued art nouveau tableware, including specialist-stylised claret jugs and lady-figure, silver-plated pewter and glass centrepieces—also trays, serving dishes and the famous Echo Mirror, which, when in good condition, still commands four-figure top prices and is considered to be investment grade.

It is interesting to note, in retrospect, from our prospective, that the 'stylised lady figure' emblems which were most likely considered 'daring' and 'risqué' in 1905, and amounted to approximately *only* 10 per cent of the whole catalogue, (the remainder appearing classical Bavarian in style), have actually become the most collectible. Such is the fascinating nature of antiques.

1.8 RARE AND VINTAGE GUITARS

And now we also have a top vintage collector's item to add: primarily, vintage Gibson and Fender Stratocasters dating back to the 1930s and 1940s through to the1970s and early 1980s, which celebrate the romantic and nostalgic rock and roll era. This iconic period, probably unsurpassed, includes such legends as Elvis Presley, Buddy Holly, the Beatles, the Rolling Stones, Cream, Led Zeppelin, Yes, Pink Floyd, Deep Purple, Genesis, Bob Dylan, the Everly Brothers, the Shadows, and Roy Orbison. Please excuse me if I have not named your favourites, as the list is long and inexhaustible, and it is notable that many of these idols are still performing and playing their iconic vintage guitars today.

That having been said, one little known fact which initially affected prices of vintage guitars was that they, in tandem with some other high value merchandise items , were originally purchased in the 1970's and 1980's as cash cows to hide (launder) monies derived from illegal pursuits such as drugs and crime. This had the effect of significantly inflating prices.

Fender Stratocaster Fiesta Red 1964

Les Paul Standard Gold Top 1954

Gibson Es-175d Sunburst 1956 Arch-Top

Gibson Sg Junior
Cherry Red 1964

Acoustic Gibson Sj200 Art Shop Gallery Model

Gibson Sg Junior
Cherry Red 1964

Thin Line Gibson
Es-350t Sunburst 1957

Vintage guitars have resurged again with huge popularity and desirability over the last ten to fifteen years, both worldwide and particularly here at davidjpym.com, where we currently hold stock at around one hundred fully vetted and authenticated top-quality pieces. The reason for this demand is due to the fact that the rock and roll era is now proving to be an iconic period in music history, where the quality and longevity of rock music, per se, has been demonstrated and has driven and inspired the desire of many professional and would-be guitarists to own a true vintage Gibson or Fender Stratocaster. The latter two makes are considered to be the most desirable in terms of quality and playability. They were also the first electric guitars. Gretsch and acoustic models are stocked as well by us, the full range with fantastic detailed photographs of every nut, bolt, 'dink' and patina, available to see on the website, as mentioned.

Only a limited number of guitars of that vintage were ever made and/or have survived in good condition. Remakes and new versions are always available to buy, but they will not generally command the same level of investment prices.

In line with all antiques/collector's artefacts, the main desire is to own an item as close as possible in originality and condition to the day it was first made, to maximise ultimate investment potential, and in reality, this can come down and translate to minute details. In the case of vintage guitars, this includes having the right screw(s), size and colour of wire, correctly dated pots, pick-ups, and most definitely the original ex-factory colour paint, and that it is not a later 'refin' (refinished) item. Although it was often the case, musicians and owners would sometimes change the appearance and features of their instrument to suit its playability according to their own requirements, unaware of course of future effect in terms of originality and resale. It can reduce the price unless it was originally a specially documented factory custom colour at outset and/or a customer modified guitar which has gained exclusive provenance and authenticity, as in the case of Eric Clapton's famous 'Blackie', as follows.

Eric Clapton's Famous 'Blackie' Fender Strat

One of the most popular and fascinating iconic stories in rock memorabilia history is that regarding Eric Clapton's famous 'Blackie,' an obsidian black Fender Strat which he described himself as a 'mongrel.' That term was derived from Eric having commissioned famous Nashville luthier Ted Newman Jones to construct his personal instrument from a collection of three to five Fenders he had purchased in bulk from the Sho-Bud guitar store in Nashville in the 1970s. At the time, Fender Strats, so the story goes, were only selling for around two to three hundred dollars each, so he had purchased the whole rack of stock vintage guitars at Sho-Bud at a one-time visit. After having given three various instruments to his friends Pete Townsend, Steve Winwood, and George Harrison, he had asked Newman Jones to make up his 'ultimate' instrument. He fancied a black Fender and liked the obsidian black alder body of a 1956 Strat but preferred the neck of another strong V-shaped 1957 version. Then, the pick-up, frets, scratch plate and selected other parts were co-opted from other vintage Strat versions he had collected.

He loved playing this revamped model, affectionately known as Blackie, and it became his workhorse, his scratched, dented, cigarette-stained, well-travelled and trusty favourite for about 20 years. Its first appearance was at his Rainbow Concert in 1973 and then later at the Live Aid concert in 1985. It was also used for many of his hit recordings, including 'Cocaine,' 'I Shot the Sheriff,' 'Lay Down Sally,' and 'Layla.' Blackie had been re-fretted and repaired/modified, on several 'pit-stop' visits to his technician. Eventually, the neck became dangerously thin and, having officially been retired from main duty in 1985, was only brought out on special and celebratory occasions until, in 2004, it was sold by Clapton at Christie's Auction House. This was specifically to raise money for his Crossroads Centre Antigua, which is a drug and alcohol rehabilitation and treatment centre he founded in 1997. It sold for a record $959,500 to New York Guitar Centre and gained the reputation as the world's most expensive guitar at that time. The guitar is believed to currently reside at the music retailer's flagship store at West 44th Street in New York City.

The Blackie Fender Strat still lives on through a limited number of Fender shop custom reissues which are identical to the original. Blackie also served as the template for a later Eric Clapton signature guitar, the Eric Clapton Stratocaster, which he has used as his primary axe since 1988.

This then paved the way for some of the later historic prices made at auction by guitar collections of other rock legends such as David Gilmour, the famous English guitarist, songwriter and singer for the hugely successful Pink Floyd, which he fronted for many years as well as having his own solo career. In 2011, *Rolling Stone*, the popular rock publication, voted him the 14th best guitarist of all time, and it was during this illustrious career that he played his black Stratocaster, which was auctioned for charity in 2019 for $3.9 million, making it one of the most expensive guitars sold at auction to that date.

1.9 DIAMONDS ARE FOREVER

The name 'diamond' is derived from the Greek word *asamas*, which translates as 'unconquerable.' The first known crystal formations were found in India in the fourth century BC, although earliest deposits are believed to have been formed between 90 million and 300 billion years ago at a depth of 90 to 400 miles below the Earth's surface. They were formed by the compression of carbon material at extreme temperatures. Their brilliance and aesthetically beautiful characteristics make them one of the Earth's most alluring, enduring and amazing natural treasures.

The slogan 'Diamonds are Forever' was originally launched and promoted in an advertising campaign by de Beers in 1947, and since then it has also been hailed as the ultimate symbol of everlasting love in engagement rings with diamonds, commanding 78% of the market. Today, also, because of recently discovered new deposits in Botswana and other African countries, diamond mining is a very significant life force providing significant income, sustenance, houses and education for previously impoverished and deprived nations since the 1970s. There are reports that sources of diamonds are depleting, with only 20% of the rough material mined suitable for gemstone and only 2% of that investment grade. The remaining 80% is used for industrial purposes such as drills and cutting machinery, due to its superior hardness.

As detailed in Volume I of *A Beginner's Guide*, the GIA (Gemological Institute of America) introduced the '4 C's' guide to assessing diamond quality in the 1950s:

- Cut
- Colour
- Clarity
- Carat weight (size)

Under this system, the following are considered optimum quality:

- the highest colour grading starts at D, which is near colourless, almost glass-like
- as near white is best in terms of colour
- an 'IF', internally flawless
- and VVS1 or VVS2 'very slightly included' clarity

Then, the larger the diamond weight (measured in carats), the greater price value, bearing in mind adherence as much as possible to the overall characteristics of the rough, mentioned above.

The 'Big 4,' the most desired and expensive world gemstones consists of:

- Diamonds
- Rubies
- Emeralds
- Sapphires

Now, in the view of experts, these have been joined by tanzanite. Tanzanite, ofttimes referred to as the 'Millennium Stone,' is a more recently discovered gemstone, first appearing in Tanzania in 1967. It is rumoured to have been formed by a single extreme 'lightening-type' force of nature, and hence it has not been

Sapphire and Diamond 'target' style ring with central 2ct diamond solitaire

Diamond Solitaire ring with 2-3 cts central diamond

Emerald and diamond 'target' style ring

9cts tanzanite, emerald-cut flanked by 3 individual brilliant-cut diamonds either side

2ct Diamond Solitaire with individual brilliant set diamonds in a square setting

Ruby and diamond 'target' style

found anywhere else since. The present mine measures just seven kilometres long by two kilometres wide. In its natural form, this zoisite gemstone exhibits a brownish-red hue, which when heated, turns to vivid blue/deep mauve to lilac with flashes of crimson, due to its strong trichroic influences reacting to different light sources. It generally exhibits strong brilliance and excellent clarity, with fine examples quite often resembling high-quality blue sapphires upon first glance.

As this phenomenal gemstone has only been discovered in one area of Tanzania, near the Merelani Hills, it is considered to be one thousand times rarer than a diamond and is becoming even more so each day. This is due to the impact of having been mined exhaustively since first discovery and the consequent depletion of sections of the total mining area.

In terms of fine jewellery, it goes without saying that the finer the gemstone quality, coupled with exquisite, superior workmanship and design detail, the higher an individual item's value. This will also entail date of manufacture and precious metals used – for example, platinum, yellow gold, white gold, or silver. Certain designs can carry a premium due to famous ownership, maker's name, and/or authentication. Names such as Tiffany, Cartier, Garrard, Bulgari, and Fabergé are celebrated for their design detail and exquisite workmanship. Also considered is design provenance, such as fine calibre settings and overall aesthetic detail as displayed in art deco 'target' style rings, which are highly regarded and desirable. Fashion and trends in antique and retro jewellery are also important.

SECTION II

Business Tips and Suggestions

2.1 BUSINESS SET-UP

By all accounts, sound advice would always be steady but sure – that is, strong foundations need to be established to enable strong building blocks and secure growth of a successful business. This is in tandem with any business start-up of whatever nature. Then the business needs to build step by step, slowly but securely, establishing strong business ethics, links and procedures. One mistake often made by a person(s) eager to start a new business is unnecessary buying and investment into props and artefacts to make the business look good. There is only one thing that matters in business, your end product, which will be the product you will be selling. In the case of antiques, that is your stock. The need to establish marketability is key, whilst endeavouring to keep costs and overheads low.

2.2 MARKET RESEARCH

In the first instance, dipping one's toe in the water on a part-time basis, to sample sales and ascertain market potential, can be achieved with either a pop-up market stall at a trades fair or renting a shop unit within an antiques arcade, as suggested in *A Beginner's Guide, Volume I.* In the book it was suggested that following your own interests of a collection or particular historic period could be a good starting point. Previous chapters of this book describe groupings of artefacts generally available in the marketplace. Of course, that potential buying ground is inexhaustible, extensive and unquantifiable because so many unique and interesting artefacts were made in Britain alone in the Victorian period. Also, the popular trend of Georgian and Victorian aristocracy travelling to Europe on the 'Grand Tour' meant that many important and stunningly beautiful items and paintings attributed to celebrated grand masters were brought back to decorate and adorn fine country houses. Britain became known in the early days of antiques trading in the 1960s and 1970s as the 'Antiques Treasure House of the World,' as fresh and original items began emerging to the marketplace from country houses.

Although some of that treasure trove has been sifted, dispersed and diluted by worldwide sales and exports over the past decades, the marketplace has a tendency to replenish by re-importing and the re-releasing of private collections at probate or the desire to capitalise on accrued values of established collections. The antiques trade is still alive and thriving today in the UK, with different developing countries and other key European and American countries keen and eager to visit, search and purchase our history, and we too theirs, of course.

2.3 PITCHING AND PRICING

Copious books and articles have been written on almost every subject and are readily available in libraries or second-hand, giving in-depth information into many groups and individual items. They also record historic and more recent prices of individual items. All that, coupled with the internet and auction house catalogues, provides extensive and immediate information. However, knowledge and experience are ultimately key in the industry, and a dealer will build his own unique ubiquitous repertoire over many years. In particular, actual direct retail prices can differ quite significantly from insurance estimates and auction prices. This is because the open market will dictate what, ultimately, a buyer is willing to pay for an item.

2.4 RENTS AND EXPENSES

Once a commitment has been made to enter the retail arena, there will be overheads and expenses which need to be factored at all times, most likely monthly, at least in terms of shop rentals, websites, online fees and travelling, aside from one's own domestic living costs. Therefore, even as a part-time hobbyist or enthusiast, these costs need to be covered and assessed, as they will become a driving force to securing sales.

2.5 SALES

Sales are the ultimate (and necessary) buzz factor of a retail business. If sales do not occur in sufficient volumes to at least cover costs but also potentially provide profit, the business will not be economically viable, unless a trader is willing to write off those expenses as being spent on the enjoyment of a hobby. To this end, for business purposes, if sufficient sales have not been achieved, and in order to encourage and fund more sales (growth), it would be advisable to try to expand your product range and/or adapt sales items towards customer preferences rather than personal leanings. The groupings described previously in this book give an indication of the types of items available for purchase at auction, house clearances, antiques fairs and so on.

2.6 ESTABLISHING BUSINESS

Experimentation will, in the first instance, be vital to establish a viable market and identity. A dealer's own preferences and leanings can initially provide inroads, but sometimes, in practice, they are found to be too limiting, unprofitable or unpopular. It will be necessary to reassess and restructure. This is where some knowledge of markets and trends can be advantageous and even help identifying a gap in the market.

2.7 BOOK-KEEPING AND RECORDS

Properly administered books, records and procedures need to be established early on to ensure an ongoing detailed resume for taxation purposes. Also as a prerequisite, and administrative tool for provision of a professional service to customers, it may be advisable to seek professional advice initially and also an accountant might be employed. The extent of these services will depend on the size and nature of individual businesses.

2.8 GROWING BUSINESS

It is necessary to build and invest in stock by the replacement of sold items and reinvestment of profits. Therefore, new acquisitions should always be considered, with careful attention not only to an item's preferential purchase price (including auction buyer's commissions), but also travel expenses and any repair or restoration costs. To build a successful business, a general upward progressive trend is desirable, as well as maintaining stock and keeping sell-on losses and breakages to an absolute minimum.

Beware being side-tracked purely by the 'glamour' of being a shop owner or dealer and rushing to take on an expensive shop lease and all associated business expenses until a clear proven business plan and technique can be forged. Living within a purchased joint shop and residential house is still a preferred business way of life for many, as it provides permanent direct access, improved onsite security and greater time-usage flexibility and benefits in quiet times. However, that aside, and the fact that the owner is then tied day and night to the business, with other possible limitations of High Street location per se, there are other less invasive opportunities such as boot sales, antique fairs and antique centres, as described in '*A Beginner's Guide' Volume I.*

Antique centres, whilst perhaps encouraging more competition (and jealousies) amongst stallholders, can sometimes promote better footfall and help to relieve tied responsibilities of being a shop owner such as staff employment and paying business rates and rentals. However, more direct competition from other stallholders within an antiques centre will necessitate a unique selling point, competitively priced stock and niche branding, to stand out from the crowd. This is especially the case if running a professional business as opposed to part-time hobby.

Over time, expansion will help to enlarge a business, if used wisely, that is a larger floor area in general, should facilitate larger stock ownership which, in turn, should then provide pro rata return on investment. As the business grows, there are direct tax advantages as rents and leases can be offset as a business expense.

However, it is important that new stock should always be sourced wisely, not just to fill or pad out shelves. Space is at a premium. Remember, each purchase of new stock is an investment of one's own hard-earned cash.

The wise and experienced dealer will often develop liaisons with trusted trade suppliers and contacts or runners who know his or her business needs and preferences, and with whom they will arrange to meet at regular intervals to browse, inspect and negotiate individual items at a more relaxed pace. Such liaisons can be beneficial to both parties saving valuable time and leg-work and can form different inter-trading tier opportunities and expansion.

2.9 CUSTOMER SATISFACTION

The best way to build a successful business is by accruing customer rapport and satisfaction, so that a considered reputation of quality, fair-dealing and reliability is achieved over a period of time and a returning regular client-base may be formed.

2.10 TRADE LOSSES

There will always be bad impulse buys, especially at auction, when, even having followed 'the rules,' being caught up in the moment and having to think quickly, the hammer goes down, you are the 'winner' and you think 'Oh no, that was a bad buy!' or 'I have paid too much!' You are then left with the onerous task of having to pass the item on quickly with no profit, perhaps even a loss, or having it linger on shelves in the hope of better days! It has to be said, however, often damaged, 'bad buys' and 'non-starters' from one dealer will find their way back into auction, but because ultimately, in the industry, 'one man's poison is another man's meat', the overall antiques pot, as a whole, exists for circulation and everyone's taking.

2.11 EBB & FLOW

There are still ‘Lovejoy’ moments when a ‘sleeper’ or unknown item is presented ‘cold’ into the market and a dealer will utilise his knowledge or instinct to know its make-up, age or quality belying its value. At these rare moments, shivers run down the spine, adrenaline and excitement start to flow, and you try to look composed whilst negotiating the ‘beneficial’ deal. But, alas, nowadays those moments are rather too few and far between due to increased public knowledge and awareness, but they can still happen, and it is also those moments which inspire dealers to travel endlessly and continuously in search of new treasure. Once the thrill of this experience has been tasted, you will probably want more, and even more when you experience your first sales and the smell of money (or success). You will have been bitten by ‘the bug.’

But there are also quiet, more mundane days when books need to be produced or stock needs rearranging/cleaning. Otherwise, you may be travelling at two o’clock in the morning in freezing-cold weather to an antiques fair, boot fair or auction, often in open air, cattle shed or other impromptu environment, where there is absolutely no guarantee of success. But doesn’t that still beat sitting in an office and having freedom to explore and manage one’s own affairs? There can be long waiting periods between lots at an auction or periods of inactivity between sales at one’s shop or trade stand, sometimes likened to sitting in war trenches. Then when it does happen, it all happens at once for a brief period of intense, adrenaline-packed bargaining and activity, and then back to quiet again.

It’s the ebb and flow, one minute up and the next down, with still no guarantee of increased sales or permanent long-term business. That is the name of the game. But once a trader or entrepreneur, it is unlikely you will ever want to return to 9am to 5pm. Also, over time, some bread-and-butter trade skills can be established to help sustain and stabilise the business, or they may have been there all along from a previous training or business environment.

2.12 BREAD AND BUTTER

These are established professional skills, such as horology (clock and watch repairs and restoration), and jewellery or furniture restoration, which enable services to be provided in conjunction and supplemental to a retail business, thus providing invaluable additional income. Also, sometimes a shop owner may sublet retail units and/or work as a sales assistant or porter at another retail establishment to earn direct income.

2.13 MAINTAINING BUSINESS

In general, once a trading pattern is established and you have discovered the key to your own unique niche area, that trend will continue, unless of course some items become unfavourable or unfashionable, and then you will need to rethink and reassess. You will always need to be open to change and in order, if desired, to enter that illusive big league, it would be advisable to keep abreast of worldwide events, market trends and investments to anticipate or even pre-empt and pre-estimate trends and fashions.

2.14 'WORKING' BUSINESS

Akin to many businesses, rewards are related to the amount of effort expended. Valued time and energy employed to search out, restore and present desirable objects will reap best rewards in the long term.

It is safe to say that a driven dealer will virtually eat and sleep antiques, whether sourcing, researching, advertising or direct selling his hard-fought and won beloved items. And nothing beats meeting a dealer face-to-face to receive full facts at a retail establishment, which is called 'fronting' business. A well-established dealer may have many varied strings to his/her bow, so that when one avenue falls quiet, another will invariably spring into action and so forth.

2.15 FRONTING BUSINESS

There is no doubt that fronting one's own business will provide the best sales figures. However, not everyone will have the time or inclination to do so. It can be quite a daunting prospect for someone who has had no direct sales experience or wishes to remain anonymous, especially in the early days of a business start-up. That is when renting a shop unit in an antiques arcade or sublet establishment can be particularly advantageous, as grouped sales are usually conducted through a central desk system when individual dealers do not need to be present.

2.16 CASH FLOW AND INVESTMENT

Dealers are advised to be astute when investing cash, especially as it is essentially their own. Best advice would be to set aside an initial sum for business start-up, investment into stock, requisite tools and business items aside from their own personal household and living expenses. That sum will then be worked and reinvested, with profits, to achieve growth over time. Care and balance needs to be achieved when paying oneself a monthly salary, alongside rentals and expenses to determine reinvestment levels.

2.17 KEY TO SUCCESS

Always have in mind new ideas and ways to improve your business, whether introducing new product lines or revamping existing ones. Restless activity and a desire to succeed, apart from inertly tiring oneself, will also have the effect of spurring the soul on to continuously wanting to achieve bigger and better things. Setting targets of growth and productivity are also paramount to being self-employed. Although, let us not forget that one of the great advantages of dealing in antiques is that each unique and individual dealer will be able to decide his/her own level of involvement, whether part-time hobbyist, collector or full-time professional. The potential scope and mixes of involvement are endless. Also, one of the biggest advantages of dealing in antiques, apart from satisfying an insatiable desire to be a collectorholic and own and handle beautiful and rare items, of course, is that they can then be resold. In theory, if one applies a wide rule of thumb that the items bought are quality items that you would not mind holding if they do not sell, it is a win/win situation. The key as a dealer is not getting too carried away and keeping within the framework of the business.

2.18 WIN/WIN DEALS

I always say that the best deals are those deals where each person wins – that is, the buyer is able to negotiate a below-market beneficial price, and the seller, having purchased the item carefully, is still able to make a reasonable profit. Win/win!

SECTION III

Top Ten Ideal Requisites to Succeed

IN THE FIRST VOLUME OF *A Beginner's Guide to Becoming an Antiques Dealer*, there were general tips and background information to help start a business as a hobby, part-time or full-time. This edition is designed to move you to the next level in terms of recommendations for providing a longer-term business.

Here are ten possible suggestions of requisites needed to succeed:

1. **An eye for a bargain:** This skill will generally develop with experience of a chosen marketplace, dipping one's toe in the water, watching and observing sale prices at auction and generally getting involved in the industry as described in Volume I.
2. **A keen sense of quality, style, beauty and workmanship:** Again, skills obtained over time of being able to assess and ascertain qualities and values of individual items.
3. **Visionary sales and marketing potential:** Ideally being able to spot a gap in the market and/or trialling various artefacts to test sales potential.
4. **Business knowledge:** Having some working experience of business or retail. Any previous experience in corporate or commercial industries will often provide valuable insights, but again, first-hand experience of being involved, ideally at the beginning, as a hobby will pave the way.
5. **Back-up restorative or engineering skills:** These can be learnt along the way as necessary, but generally being able to 'add value' or restore an item will improve and enhance the sales price. Often, researched professional cleaning skills will serve to promote an item's optimum presentation potential, taking care not to over-polish or use dangerous solvents and cleaners. If in doubt, best to leave as is.
6. **Sales/negotiation:** Fronting and personally representing an owned business can serve to establish good relations and optimum performance and sales.

7. **Determination:** Having ultimate control of one's own fortunes will encourage 101% commitment, as all efforts are now solely invested in your own success.
8. **Energy/self-motivation:** Ideal requisites to maintain and progress in a successful professional business.
9. **Resourcefulness and ability to change direction as necessary:** When one avenue fails, there are always other options to pursue, particularly in the case of antiques, where trends and fashion often serve to dictate the success and performance of individual sales items.
10. **Money for investment:** Always a factor in determining each person's involvement and stockholding.

But remember, the beauty of the antiques industry is that *anyone* can enter and choose the level at which he or she wishes to be involved either as a part-time hobby or full-time professional business.

In Conclusion

A Thing Of Beauty Is A Joy Forever

IN TERMS OF BUYING AND selling antiques, to try to achieve the optimum quality of a product, it should be as near possible to its *original* condition in colour, decoration and unmodified totality of design, structure and finish as when first manufactured. In that way, its authenticity cannot be challenged or questioned and should then translate into the best achievable price for investment purposes. In general terms, an item which was quality-built at conception will continue to achieve and accrue relative values and demand in line with investment. 'Quality always sells' is a well-known saying and well-coined phrase.

Fashions and trends will also play a part. However, there are many unique, quirky and fascinating items which reflect a country's changing time periods and associated fashion trends, which will always provide enthralling fascination and joy, whether antique, contemporary, retro, vintage or eclectic. Family heirlooms of whatever value carry unparalleled and unquantified emotional memories.

It is only in the case of fully verified and documented proven ownership, such as in the case of vintage guitars, where an instrument has sometimes been customised and modified to suit the playability and unique requirements of a famous owner, that an item may have attained extra celebrity status and value.

The illustrious art market is also a vast, fascinating subject area requiring extensive verification and meticulous authentication, steeped in history and reputations of grand masters and acclaimed artists over centuries and antique periods.

At the end of the day, it all boils down to market value and how much the market dictates the buying public is prepared to pay to own pieces of our wonderful, rich history. There are still many undiscovered treasures not only buried within the Earth but hidden in cupboards and attics or simply undervalued, arriving in boot fairs, auctions or house sales. So, from metal detecting, surfing the net, buying and selling, the National Trust, and archaeological discoveries, the UK alone is revered and envied for its love of history and heritage. There is also homage and appreciation in many other countries for all things natural, historical and cultural, and ultimately—we all love a bargain!

I hope you found this book interesting, useful and inspiring. Please enjoy, and happy antiques hunting.

Review Requested:

We'd like to know if you enjoyed the book. Please consider leaving a review on the platform from which you purchased the book.

Lightning Source UK Ltd.
Milton Keynes UK
UKHW051946270622
405027UK00006B/95